THE WASTE LAND
AND SELECTED POEMS

by
T. S. ELIOT

COMPASS CIRCLE

The Waste Land And Selected Poems.
Current edition published by Compass Circle in 2019.

Published by Compass Circle
A Division of Garcia & Kitzinger Pty Ltd
Cover copyright ©2019 by Compass Circle.

All rights reserved. No part of this publication may be reproduced, stored in a retrieval system, or transmitted, in any form or by any means, electronic, mechanical, photocopying, recording or otherwise without the prior permission of the publisher.

Note:
All efforts have been made to preserve original spellings and punctuation of the original edition which may include old-fashioned English spellings of words and archaic variants.

This book is a product of its time and does not reflect the same views on race, gender, sexuality, ethnicity, and interpersonal relations as it would if it were written today.

For information contact :
information@compass-circle.com

Only those who will risk going too far can possibly find out how far one can go

T. S. ELIOT

SECRET WISDOM OF THE AGES SERIES

Life presents itself, it advances in a fast way. Life indeed never stops. It never stops until the end. The most diverse questions peek and fade in our minds. Sometimes we seek for answers. Sometimes we just let time go by.

The book you have now in your hands has been waiting to be discovered by you. This book may reveal the answers to some of your questions.

Books are friends. Friends who are always by your side and who can give you great ideas, advice or just comfort your soul.

A great book can make you see things in your soul that you have not yet discovered, make you see things in your soul that you were not aware of.

Great books can change your life for the better. They can make you understand fascinating theories, give you new ideas, inspire you to undertake new challenges or to walk along new paths.

Literature Classics like the one of *The Waste Land And Selected Poems* are indeed a secret to many, but for those of us lucky enough to have discovered them, by one way or another, these books can enlighten us. They can open a wide range of possibilities to us. Because achieving greatness requires knowledge.

The series SECRET WISDOM OF THE AGES presented by Compass Circle try to bring you the great timeless masterpieces of literature, autobiographies and personal development,.

We welcome you to discover with us fascinating works by Nathaniel Hawthorne, Sir Arthur Conan Doyle, Edith Wharton, among others.

Contents

I The Waste Land — 2
   I.   The Burial of the Dead — 3
   II.   A Game of Chess — 7
   III.   The Fire Sermon — 12
   IV.   Death by Water — 18
   V.   What the Thunder Said — 19

II Other Selected Poems — 31
Gerontion — 32
Le Directeur — 35
Mr. Eliot's Sunday Morning Service — 36
Portrait of a Lady — 38
Morning at the Window — 43
The Boston Evening Transcript — 44
Aunt Helen — 45
Cousin Nancy — 46
Mr. Apollinax — 47
Conversation Galante — 48
Hysteria — 49

Part I

The Waste Land

I

The Burial of the Dead

A PRIL is the cruellest month, breeding
Lilacs out of the dead land, mixing
Memory and desire, stirring
Dull roots with spring rain.
Winter kept us warm, covering
Earth in forgetful snow, feeding
A little life with dried tubers.
Summer surprised us, coming over the Starnbergersee
With a shower of rain; we stopped in the colonnade,
And went on in sunlight, into the Hofgarten,

And drank coffee, and talked for an hour.
Bin gar keine Russin, stamm' aus Litauen, echt deutsch.
And when we were children, staying at the archduke's,
My cousin's, he took me out on a sled,
And I was frightened. He said, Marie,
Marie, hold on tight. And down we went.
In the mountains, there you feel free.
I read, much of the night, and go south in the winter.

What are the roots that clutch, what branches grow
Outof this stony rubbish? Son of man, 20

You cannot say, or guess, for you know only
A heap of broken images, where the sun beats,
And the dead tree gives no shelter, the cricket no relief,
And the dry stone no sound of water. Only
There is shadow under this red rock,
(Come in under the shadow of this red rock),
And I will show you something different from either
Your shadow at morning striding behind you
Or your shadow at evening rising to meet you;
I will show you fear in a handful of dust. 30

> *Frisch weht der Wind*
> *Der Heimat zu,*
> *Mein Irisch Kind,*
> *Wo weilest du?*

"You gave me hyacinths first a year ago;
"They called me the hyacinth girl."
—Yet when we came back, late, from the Hyacinth
    garden,
Your arms full, and your hair wet, I could not
Speak, and my eyes failed, I was neither
Living nor dead, and I knew nothing, 40
Looking into the heart of light, the silence.

Od' und leer das Meer.

Madame Sosostris, famous clairvoyante,
Had a bad cold, nevertheless

Is known to be the wisest woman in Europe,
With a wicked pack of cards. Here, said she,
Is your card, the drowned Phoenician Sailor,
(Those are pearls that were his eyes. Look!)
Here is Belladonna, the Lady of the Rocks,
50 The lady of situations.
Here is the man with three staves, and here the Wheel,

And here is the one-eyed merchant, and this card,
Which is blank, is something he carries on his back,
Which I am forbidden to see. I do not find
The Hanged Man. Fear death by water.
I see crowds of people, walking round in a ring.
Thank you. If you see dear Mrs. Equitone,
Tell her I bring the horoscope myself:
One must be so careful these days.

60 Unreal City,
Under the brown fog of a winter dawn,

A crowd flowed over London Bridge, so many,
I had not thought death had undone so many.
Sighs, short and infrequent, were exhaled,
And each man fixed his eyes before his feet.
Flowed up the hill and down King William Street,
To where Saint Mary Woolnoth kept the hours
With a dead sound on the final stroke of nine.
There I saw one I knew, and stopped him, crying
   "Stetson!
70 "You who were with me in the ships at Mylae!

"That corpse you planted last year in your garden,
"Has it begun to sprout? Will it bloom this year?
"Or has the sudden frost disturbed its bed?
"Oh keep the Dog far hence, that's friend to men,
"Or with his nails he'll dig it up again!
"You! hypocrite lecteur!—mon semblable,—mon frère!"

II

A Game of Chess

THE Chair she sat in, like a burnished throne,
   Glowed on the marble, where the glass
   Held up by standards wrought with fruited
vines
80 From which a golden Cupidon peeped out
(Another hid his eyes behind his wing)
Doubled the flames of sevenbranched candelabra
Reflecting light upon the table as
The glitter of her jewels rose to meet it,
From satin cases poured in rich profusion;

In vials of ivory and coloured glass
Unstoppered, lurked her strange synthetic perfumes,
Unguent, powdered, or liquid—troubled, confused
And drowned the sense in odours; stirred by the air
90 That freshened from the window, these ascended
In fattening the prolonged candle-flames,
Flung their smoke into the laquearia,
Stirring the pattern on the coffered ceiling.
Huge sea-wood fed with copper
Burned green and orange, framed by the

coloured stone,
In which sad light a carvèd dolphin swam.

Above the antique mantel was displayed
As though a window gave upon the sylvan scene
The change of Philomel, by the barbarous king
So rudely forced; yet there the nightingale   100
Filled all the desert with inviolable voice
And still she cried, and still the world pursues,
"Jug Jug" to dirty ears.
And other withered stumps of time
Were told upon the walls; staring forms
Leaned out, leaning, hushing the room enclosed.
Footsteps shuffled on the stair.

Under the firelight, under the brush, her hair
Spread out in fiery points
Glowed into words, then would be savagely still.   110

"My nerves are bad tonight. Yes, bad. Stay with me.
"Speak to me. Why do you never speak? Speak.
"What are you thinking of? What thinking? What?
"I never know what you are thinking. Think."

I think we are in rats' alley
Where the dead men lost their bones.

"What is that noise?"
                    The wind under the door.
"What is that noise now? What is the wind doing?"
                    Nothing again nothing.   120

                              "Do
"You know nothing? Do you see nothing? Do you re-
member
"Nothing?"
    I remember
Those are pearls that were his eyes.
"Are you alive, or not? Is there nothing in your head?"
                              But

O O O O that Shakespeherian Rag—
It's so elegant
130 So intelligent

"What shall I do now? What shall I do?"
"I shall rush out as I am, and walk the street
"With my hair down, so. What shall we do tomorrow?
"What shall we ever do?"
                    The hot water at ten.
And if it rains, a closed car at four.
And we shall play a game of chess,
Pressing lidless eyes and waiting for a knock upon
    the door.

When Lil's husband got demobbed, I said—

140 I didn't mince my words, I said to her myself,
HURRY UP PLEASE ITS TIME
Now Albert's coming back, make yourself a bit smart.
He'll want to know what you done with that money he
gave you
To get yourself some teeth. He did, I was there.
You have them all out, Lil, and get a nice set,

He said, I swear, I can't bear to look at you.
And no more can't I, I said, and think of poor Albert,
He's been in the army four years, he wants a good time,

And if you don't give it him, there's others will, I said.
Oh is there, she said. Something o' that, I said.   150
Then I'll know who to thank, she said, and give me a straight look.
HURRY UP PLEASE ITS TIME
If you don't like it you can get on with it, I said,
Others can pick and choose if you can't.
But if Albert makes off, it won't be for lack of telling.
You ought to be ashamed, I said, to look so antique.
(And her only thirty-one.)
I can't help it, she said, pulling a long face,

It's them pills I took, to bring it off, she said.
(She's had five already, and nearly died of   160
    young George.)
The chemist said it would be alright, but I've never been the same.
You *are* a proper fool, I said.
Well, if Albert wont leave you alone, there it is, I said,
What you get married for if you dont want children?
HURRY UP PLEASE ITS TIME
Well, that Sunday Albert was home, they had a hot gammon,
And they asked me in to dinner, to get the beauty of it hot—

HURRY UP PLEASE ITS TIME
HURRY UP PLEASE ITS TIME

170 Goonight Bill. Goonight Lou. Goonight May. Goonight.
Ta ta. Goonight. Goonight.
Good night, ladies, good night, sweet ladies, good night, good night.

III

The Fire Sermon

THE river's tent is broken: the last fingers
     of leaf
     Clutch and sink into the wet bank. The wind
Crosses the brown land, unheard. The nymphs
     are departed.
Sweet Thames, run softly, till I end my song.
The river bears no empty bottles, sandwich papers,
Silk handkerchiefs, cardboard boxes, cigarette ends
Or other testimony of summer nights. The nymphs
     are departed.

And their friends, the loitering heirs of city directors;   180
Departed, have left no addresses.
By the waters of Leman I sat down and wept . . .
Sweet Thames, run softly till I end my song,
Sweet Thames, run softly, for I speak not loud or long.
But at my back in a cold blast I hear
The rattle of the bones, and chuckle spread from ear
     to ear.

The Waste Land

A rat crept softly through the vegetation
Dragging its slimy belly on the bank
While I was fishing in the dull canal

190 On a winter evening round behind the gashouse.
Musing upon the king my brother's wreck
And on the king my father's death before him.
White bodies naked on the low damp ground
And bones cast in a little low dry garret,
Rattled by the rat's foot only, year to year.
But at my back from time to time I hear
The sound of horns and motors, which shall bring
Sweeney to Mrs. Porter in the spring.
O the moon shone bright on Mrs. Porter
200 And on her daughter

They wash their feet in soda water
Et, O ces voix d'enfants, chantant dans la coupole!

Twit twit twit
Jug jug jug jug jug jug
So rudely forc'd.
Tereu

Unreal City
Under the brown fog of a winter noon
Mr. Eugenides, the Smyrna merchant
210 Unshaven, with a pocket full of currants
C.i.f. London: documents at sight,
Asked me in demotic French
To luncheon at the Cannon Street Hotel

Followed by a weekend at the Metropole.

At the violet hour, when the eyes and back
Turn upward from the desk, when the human engine waits
Like a taxi throbbing waiting,
I Tiresias, though blind, throbbing between two lives,
Old man with wrinkled female breasts, can see
At the violet hour, the evening hour that strives   220
Homeward, and brings the sailor home from sea,
The typist home at teatime, clears her breakfast, lights

Her stove, and lays out food in tins.
Out of the window perilously spread
Her drying combinations touched by the sun's last rays,
On the divan are piled (at night her bed)
Stockings, slippers, camisoles, and stays.
I Tiresias, old man with wrinkled dugs
Perceived the scene, and foretold the rest—
I too awaited the expected guest.   230
He, the young man carbuncular, arrives,
A small house agent's clerk, with one bold stare,
One of the low on whom assurance sits
As a silk hat on a Bradford millionaire.
The time is now propitious, as he guesses,
The meal is ended, she is bored and tired,

Endeavours to engage her in caresses
Which still are unreproved, if undesired.
Flushed and decided, he assaults at once;
Exploring hands encounter no defence;   240

His vanity requires no response,
And makes a welcome of indifference.
(And I Tiresias have foresuffered all
Enacted on this same divan or bed;
I who have sat by Thebes below the wall
And walked among the lowest of the dead.)
Bestows one final patronising kiss,
And gropes his way, finding the stairs unlit . . .

She turns and looks a moment in the glass,
250 Hardly aware of her departed lover;

Her brain allows one half-formed thought to pass:
"Well now that's done: and I'm glad it's over."
When lovely woman stoops to folly and
Paces about her room again, alone,
She smoothes her hair with automatic hand,
And puts a record on the gramophone.

"This music crept by me upon the waters"
And along the Strand, up Queen Victoria Street.
O City city, I can sometimes hear
260 Beside a public bar in Lower Thames Street,

The pleasant whining of a mandoline
And a clatter and a chatter from within
Where fishmen lounge at noon: where the walls
Of Magnus Martyr hold
Inexplicable splendour of Ionian white and gold.

The river sweats
Oil and tar
The barges drift
With the turning tide
Red sails   270
Wide
To leeward, swing on the heavy spar.
The barges wash

Drifting logs
Down Greenwich reach
Past the Isle of Dogs.
          Weialala leia
            Wallala leialala
Elizabeth and Leicester
Beating oars   280
The stern was formed
A gilded shell
Red and gold
The brisk swell
Rippled both shores
Southwest wind
Carried down stream
The peal of bells
White towers

          Weialala leia   290
            Wallala leialala
"Trams and dusty trees.
Highbury bore me. Richmond and Kew
Undid me. By Richmond I raised my knees

Supine on the floor of a narrow canoe."

"My feet are at Moorgate, and my heart
Under my feet. After the event
He wept. He promised 'a new start.'
I made no comment. What should I resent?"
"On Margate Sands.
I can connect
Nothing with nothing.

The broken fingernails of dirty hands.
My people humble people who expect
Nothing."
           la la

To Carthage then I came

Burning burning burning burning
O Lord Thou pluckest me out
O Lord Thou pluckest

burning

IV

Death by Water

PHLEBAS the Phoenician, a fortnight dead,
Forgot the cry of gulls, and the deep sea swell
And the profit and loss.
                        A current under sea
Picked his bones in whispers. As he rose and fell
He passed the stages of his age and youth
Entering the whirlpool.
                        Gentile or Jew
O you who turn the wheel and look to windward,   320
Consider Phlebas, who was once handsome and tall
   as you.

V

What the Thunder Said

A FTER the torchlight red on sweaty faces
After the frosty silence in the gardens
After the agony in stony places
The shouting and the crying
Prison and palace and reverberation
Of thunder of spring over distant mountains
He who was living is now dead
We who were living are now dying
With a little patience

Here is no water but only rock
Rock and no water and the sandy road

The road winding above among the mountains
Which are mountains of rock without water
If there were water we should stop and drink
Amongst the rock one cannot stop or think
Sweat is dry and feet are in the sand
If there were only water amongst the rock
Dead mount in mouth of carious teeth that cannot spit
Here one can neither stand nor lie nor sit

There is not even silence in the mountains

But dry sterile thunder without rain
There is not even solitude in the mountains
But red sullen faces sneer and snarl
From doors of mudcracked houses
                    If there were water
  And no rock
  If there were rock
  And also water
  And water
  A spring   350
  A pool among the rock
  If there were the sound of water only
  Not the cicada
  And dry grass singing
  But sound of water over a rock

Where the hermit-thrush sings in the pine trees
Drip drop drip drop drop drop drop
But there is no water

Who is the third who walks always beside you?
When I count, there are only you and I together   360
But when I look ahead up the white road
There is always another one walking beside you
Gliding wrapt in a brown mantle, hooded
I do not know whether a man or a woman
— But who is that on the other side of you?

The Waste Land

      What is that sound high in the air
      Murmur of maternal lamentation
      Who are those hooded hordes swarming
      Over endless plains, stumbling in cracked earth
370 Ringed by the flat horizon only
      What is the city over the mountains
      Cracks and reforms and bursts in the violet air
      Falling towers
      Jerusalem Athens Alexandria
      Vienna London
      Unreal

      A woman drew her long black hair out tight
      And fiddled whisper music on those strings
      And bats with baby faces in the violet light
380 Whistled, and beat their wings
      And crawled head downward down a blackened wall
      And upside down in air were towers
      Tolling reminiscent bells, that kept the hours
      And voices singing out of empty cisterns and exhausted
         wells.

      In this decayed hole among the mountains
      In the faint moonlight, the grass is singing
      Over the tumbled graves, about the chapel
      There is the empty chapel, only the wind's home.

      It has no windows, and the door swings,
390 Dry bones can harm no one.
      Only a cock stood on the rooftree

Co co rico co co rico
In a flash of lightning. Then a damp gust
Bringing rain
Ganga was sunken, and the limp leaves
Waited for rain, while the black clouds
Gathered far distant, over Himavant.
The jungle crouched, humped in silence.
Then spoke the thunder
DA   400
Datta: what have we given?
My friend, blood shaking my heart
The awful daring of a moment's surrender

Which an age of prudence can never retract
By this, and this only, we have existed
Which is not to be found in our obituaries
Or in memories draped by the beneficent spider
Or under seals broken by the lean solicitor
In our empty rooms
DA   410
Dayadhvam: I have heard the key
Turn in the door once and turn once only
We think of the key, each in his prison
Thinking of the key, each confirms a prison
Only at nightfall, aetherial rumours

Revive for a moment a broken Coriolanus
DA
Damyata: The boat responded
Gaily, to the hand expert with sail and oar
The sea was calm, your heart would have responded   420

Gaily, when invited, beating obedient
To controlling hands

                I sat upon the shore
Fishing, with the arid plain behind me
Shall I at least set my lands in order?

London Bridge is falling down falling down falling
    down

Poi s'ascose nel foco che gli affina
Quando fiam ceu chelidon— O swallow swallow
Le Prince d'Aquitaine à la tour abolie
These fragments I have shored against my ruins
Why then Ile fit you. Hieronymo's mad againe.
Datta. Dayadhvam. Damyata.

    Shantih shantih shantih

Notes

NOT only the title, but the plan and a good deal of the incidental symbolism of the poem were suggested by Miss Jessie L. Weston's book on the Grail legend: *From Ritual to Romance* (Macmillan). Indeed, so deeply am I indebted, Miss Weston's book will elucidate the difficulties of the poem much better than my notes can do; and I recommend it (apart from the great interest of the book itself) to any who think such elucidation of the poem worth the trouble. To another work of anthropology I am indebted in general, one which has influenced our generation profoundly; I mean *The Golden Bough*; I have used especially the two volumes *Atthis Adonis Osiris*. Anyone who is acquainted with these works will immediately recognise in the poem certain references to vegetation ceremonies.

I. THE BURIAL OF THE DEAD

Line 20. Cf. Ezekiel II, i.
23. Cf. Ecclesiastes XII, 5.
31. V. *Tristan und Isolde*, I, verses 5-8.
42. Id. III, verse 24.
46. I am not familiar with the exact constitution of the Tarot pack of cards, from which I have obviously departed to suit my own convenience. The Hanged Man, a member of the traditional pack, fits my purpose in two ways: because he is associated in my mind with the Hanged God of Frazer, and because I associate him with the hooded figure in the passage of the disciples to Emmaus in Part V. The Phoenician Sailor and the Merchant appear later; also the "crowds of people," and Death by Water is executed in Part IV. The Man with Three Staves (an authentic member of the Tarot pack) I associate, quite arbitrarily, with the Fisher King himself.
60. Cf. Baudelaire:
"Fourmillante cité, cité pleine de rêves,
"Où le spectre en plein jour raccroche le passant."
63. Cf. *Inferno* III, 55–57:

                "si lunga tratta
di gente, ch'io non avrei mai creduto
che morte tanta n'avesse disfatta."

64. Cf. *Inferno* IV, 25–27:

"Quivi, secondo che per ascoltare,
"non avea pianto, ma' che di sospiri,
"che l'aura eterna facevan tremare."

68. A phenomenon which I have often noticed.
74. Cf. the Dirge in Webster's *White Devil*.
76. V. Baudelaire, Preface to *Fleurs du Mal*.

II. A GAME OF CHESS

77. Cf. *Antony and Cleopatra*, II. ii., l. 190.
92. Laquearia. V. *Aeneid*, I, 726:

> dependent lychni laquearibus aureis
> incensi, et noctem flammis funalia vincunt.

98. Sylvan scene. V. Milton, *Paradise Lost*, IV, 140.
99. V. Ovid, *Metamorphoses*, VI, Philomela.
100. Cf. Part III l. 204.
115. Cf. Part III l. 195.
118. Cf. Webster: "Is the wind in that door still?"
126. Cf. Part I l. 37, 48.
138. Cf. the game of chess in Middleton's *Women beware Women*.

III. THE FIRE SERMON

176. V. Spenser, *Prothalamion*.
192. Cf. *The Tempest*, I. ii.
196. Cf. Day, *Parliament of Bees*:

"When of the sudden, listening, you shall hear,
"A noise of horns and hunting, which shall bring
"Actaeon to Diana in the spring,
"Where all shall see her naked skin..."

197. Cf. Marvell, *To His Coy Mistress*.
199. I do not know the origin of the ballad from which these lines are taken: it was reported to me from Sydney, Australia.
202. V. Verlaine, *Parsifal*.
210. The currants were quoted at a price "carriage and insurance free to London"; and the Bill of Lading etc. were to be handed to the buyer upon payment of the sight draft.
218. Tiresias, although a mere spectator and not indeed a "character," is yet the most important personage in the poem, uniting all the rest. Just as the one-eyed merchant, seller of

currants, melts into the Phoenician Sailor, and the latter is not wholly distinct from Ferdinand Prince of Naples, so all the women are one woman, and the two sexes meet in Tiresias. What Tiresias sees, in fact, is the substance of the poem. The whole passage from Ovid is of great anthropological interest:

> ... Cum Iunone iocos et maior vestra profecto est
>
> Quam, quae contingit maribus', dixisse, 'voluptas.'
> Illa negat; placuit quae sit sententia docti
> Quaerere Tiresiae: venus huic erat utraque nota.
> Nam duo magnorum viridi coeuntia silva
> Corpora serpentum baculi violaverat ictu
> Deque viro factus, mirabile, femina septem
> Egerat autumnos; octavo rursus eosdem
> Vidit et 'est vestrae si tanta potentia plagae,'
> Dixit 'ut auctoris sortem in contraria mutet,
> Nunc quoque vos feriam!' percussis anguibus isdem
> Forma prior rediit genetivaque venit imago.
> Arbiter hic igitur sumptus de lite iocosa
> Dicta Iovis firmat; gravius Saturnia iusto
> Nec pro materia fertur doluisse suique
> Iudicis aeterna damnavit lumina nocte,
> At pater omnipotens (neque enim licet inrita cuiquam
> Facta dei fecisse deo) pro lumine adempto
> Scire futura dedit poenamque levavit honore.

221. This may not appear as exact as Sappho's lines, but I had in mind the "longshore" or "dory" fisherman, who returns at nightfall.

253. V. Goldsmith, the song in *The Vicar of Wakefield*.

257. V. *The Tempest*, as above.

264. The interior of St. Magnus Martyr is to my mind one of the finest among Wren's interiors. See *The Proposed Demolition of Nineteen City Churches:* (P. S. King & Son, Ltd.).

266. The Song of the (three) Thames-daughters begins here. From line 292 to 306 inclusive they speak in turn. V. *Götterdämmerung*, III, i: the Rhinedaughters.

279. V. Froude, *Elizabeth*, Vol. I, ch. iv, letter of De Quadra to Philip of Spain:

> "In the afternoon we were in a barge, watching the games on the river. (The queen) was alone with Lord Robert and myself on the poop, when they began to talk nonsense, and went so far that Lord Robert at last said, as I was on the spot there was no reason why they should not be married if the queen pleased."

293. Cf. *Purgatorio*, V. 133:

> "Ricorditi di me, che son la Pia;
> "Siena mi fe', disfecemi Maremma."

307. V. St. Augustine's *Confessions:* "to Carthage then I came, where a cauldron of unholy loves sang all about mine ears."

308. The complete text of the Buddha's Fire Sermon (which corresponds in importance to the Sermon on the Mount) from which these words are taken, will be found translated in the late Henry Clarke Warren's *Buddhism in Translation* (Harvard Oriental Series). Mr. Warren was one of the great pioneers of Buddhist studies in the Occident.

312. From St. Augustine's *Confessions* again. The collocation of these two representatives of eastern and western asceticism, as the culmination of this part of the poem, is not an accident.

V. WHAT THE THUNDER SAID

In the first part of Part V three themes are employed: the journey to Emmaus, the approach to the Chapel Perilous (see Miss Weston's book) and the present decay of eastern Europe.

357. This is *Turdus aonalaschkae pallasii*, the hermit-thrush which I have heard in Quebec County. Chapman says (*Handbook of Birds of Eastern North America*) "it is most at home

The Waste Land

in secluded woodland and thickety retreats. . . . Its notes are not remarkable for variety or volume, but in purity and sweetness of tone and exquisite modulation they are unequalled." Its "water-dripping song" is justly celebrated.

360. The following lines were stimulated by the account of one of the Antarctic expeditions (I forget which, but I think one of Shackleton's): it was related that the party of explorers, at the extremity of their strength, had the constant delusion that there was *one more member* than could actually be counted.

366–76. Cf. Hermann Hesse, *Blick ins Chaos:* "Schon ist halb Europa, schon ist zumindest der halbe Osten Europas auf dem Wege zum Chaos, fährt betrunken im heiligem Wahn am Abgrund entlang und singt dazu, singt betrunken und hymnisch wie Dmitri Karamasoff sang. Ueber diese Lieder lacht der Bürger beleidigt, der Heilige und Seher hört sie mit Tränen."

401. "Datta, dayadhvam, damyata" (Give, sympathize, control). The fable of the meaning of the Thunder is found in the *Brihadaranyaka—Upanishad*, 5, 1. A translation is found in Deussen's *Sechzig Upanishads des Veda*, p. 489.

407. Cf. Webster, *The White Devil*, v. vi:

". . . they'll remarry
Ere the worm pierce your winding-sheet, ere the spider
Make a thin curtain for your epitaphs."

411. Cf. *Inferno*, XXXIII, 46:

"ed io sentii chiavar l'uscio di sotto
all'orribile torre."

Also F. H. Bradley, *Appearance and Reality*, p. 346.

"My external sensations are no less private to myself than are my thoughts or my feelings. In either case my experience falls within my own circle, a circle closed on the outside; and, with all its elements alike, every sphere is opaque to the others which surround it. . . . In brief, regarded as an existence which appears in a soul, the whole world for each is peculiar and private to that soul."

424. V. Weston, *From Ritual to Romance;* chapter on the Fisher King.

427. V. *Purgatorio*, XXVI, 148.

"'Ara vos prec per aquella valor
'que vos guida al som de l'escalina,
'sovegna vos a temps de ma dolor.'
Poi s'ascose nel foco che gli affina."

428. V. *Pervigilium Veneris.* Cf. Philomela in Parts II and III.

429. V. Gerard de Nerval, Sonnet *El Desdichado.*

431. V. Kyd's *Spanish Tragedy.*

434. Shantih. Repeated as here, a formal ending to an Upanishad. "The Peace which passeth understanding" is a feeble translation of the content of this word.

Part II

Other Selected Poems

Gerontion

Thou hast nor youth nor age
But as it were an after dinner sleep
Dreaming of both.

Here I am, an old man in a dry month,
Being read to by a boy, waiting for rain.
I was neither at the hot gates
Nor fought in the warm rain
Nor knee deep in the salt marsh, heaving a cutlass,   5
Bitten by flies, fought.
My house is a decayed house,
And the jew squats on the window sill, the owner,
Spawned in some estaminet of Antwerp,
Blistered in Brussels, patched and peeled in London.   10
The goat coughs at night in the field overhead;
Rocks, moss, stonecrop, iron, merds.
The woman keeps the kitchen, makes tea,
Sneezes at evening, poking the peevish gutter.

          I an old man,   15
A dull head among windy spaces.

Signs are taken for wonders. "We would see a sign":
The word within a word, unable to speak a word,
Swaddled with darkness. In the juvescence of the year
Came Christ the tiger   20

Geronion

In depraved May, dogwood and chestnut, flowering Judas,
To be eaten, to be divided, to be drunk
Among whispers; by Mr. Silvero
With caressing hands, at Limoges
Who walked all night in the next room;
By Hakagawa, bowing among the Titians;
By Madame de Tornquist, in the dark room
Shifting the candles; Fraulein von Kulp
Who turned in the hall, one hand on the door. Vacant shuttles
Weave the wind. I have no ghosts,
An old man in a draughty house
Under a windy knob.

After such knowledge, what forgiveness? Think now
History has many cunning passages, contrived corridors
And issues, deceives with whispering ambitions,
Guides us by vanities. Think now
She gives when our attention is distracted
And what she gives, gives with such supple confusions
That the giving famishes the craving. Gives too late
What's not believed in, or if still believed,
In memory only, reconsidered passion. Gives too soon
Into weak hands, what's thought can be dispensed with
Till the refusal propagates a fear. Think
Neither fear nor courage saves us. Unnatural vices
Are fathered by our heroism. Virtues
Are forced upon us by our impudent crimes.
These tears are shaken from the wrath-bearing tree.

The tiger springs in the new year. Us he devours. Think at
   last
We have not reached conclusion, when I
Stiffen in a rented house. Think at last
I have not made this show purposelessly

And it is not by any concitation
Of the backward devils.
I would meet you upon this honestly.
I that was near your heart was removed therefrom
To lose beauty in terror, terror in inquisition.
I have lost my passion: why should I need to keep it
Since what is kept must be adulterated?
I have lost my sight, smell, hearing, taste and touch:
How should I use it for your closer contact?

These with a thousand small deliberations
Protract the profit of their chilled delirium,
Excite the membrane, when the sense has cooled,
With pungent sauces, multiply variety
In a wilderness of mirrors. What will the spider do,
Suspend its operations, will the weevil
Delay? De Bailhache, Fresca, Mrs. Cammel, whirled
Beyond the circuit of the shuddering Bear
In fractured atoms. Gull against the wind, in the windy straits
Of Belle Isle, or running on the Horn,
White feathers in the snow, the Gulf claims,
And an old man driven by the Trades
To a sleepy corner.

                Tenants of the house,
Thoughts of a dry brain in a dry season.

Le Directeur

    Malheur à la malheureuse Tamise!
    Tamise! Qui coule si pres du Spectateur.
    Le directeur
    Conservateur
5   Du Spectateur
    Empeste la brise.
    Les actionnaires
    Réactionnaires
    Du Spectateur
10 Conservateur
    Bras dessus bras dessous
    Font des tours
    A pas de loup.
    Dans un égout
15 Une petite fille
    En guenilles
    Camarde
    Regarde
    Le directeur
20 Du Spectateur
    Conservateur
    Et crève d'amour.

Mr. Eliot's Sunday Morning Service

Look, look, master, here comes two religious caterpillars.

—*The Jew of Malta.*

Polyphiloprogenitive
The sapient sutlers of the Lord
Drift across the window-panes.
In the beginning was the Word.

In the beginning was the Word. 5
Superfetation of τό ἕν,
And at the mensual turn of time
Produced enervate Origen.

A painter of the Umbrian school
Designed upon a gesso ground 10
The nimbus of the Baptized God.
The wilderness is cracked and browned

But through the water pale and thin
Still shine the unoffending feet
And there above the painter set 15
The Father and the Paraclete.

. . . . .

The sable presbyters approach
The avenue of penitence;
The young are red and pustular
Clutching piaculative pence.

Under the penitential gates
Sustained by staring Seraphim
Where the souls of the devout
Burn invisible and dim.

Along the garden-wall the bees
With hairy bellies pass between
The staminate and pistilate,
Blest office of the epicene.

Sweeney shifts from ham to ham
Stirring the water in his bath.
The masters of the subtle schools
Are controversial, polymath.

Portrait of a Lady

Thou hast committed—
Fornication: but that was in another country
And besides, the wench is dead.
—The Jew of Malta.

I

AMONG the smoke and fog of a December afternoon
You have the scene arrange itself—as it will seem to do—
With "I have saved this afternoon for you";
And four wax candles in the darkened room,
Four rings of light upon the ceiling overhead,   5
An atmosphere of Juliet's tomb
Prepared for all the things to be said, or left unsaid.
We have been, let us say, to hear the latest Pole
Transmit the Preludes, through his hair and finger-tips.
"So intimate, this Chopin, that I think his soul   10
Should be resurrected only among friends
Some two or three, who will not touch the bloom
That is rubbed and questioned in the concert room."
—And so the conversation slips
Among velleities and carefully caught regrets   15
Through attenuated tones of violins
Mingled with remote cornets
And begins.

"You do not know how much they mean to me, my friends,
And how, how rare and strange it is, to find   20

Portrait of a Lady

In a life composed so much, so much of odds and ends,
(For indeed I do not love it... you knew? you are not blind!
How keen you are!)
To find a friend who has these qualities,
25 Who has, and gives
Those qualities upon which friendship lives.
How much it means that I say this to you—
Without these friendships—life, what *cauchemar!*"
Among the windings of the violins
30 And the ariettes
Of cracked cornets
Inside my brain a dull tom-tom begins
Absurdly hammering a prelude of its own,
Capricious monotone
35 That is at least one definite "false note."
—Let us take the air, in a tobacco trance,
Admire the monuments
Discuss the late events,
Correct our watches by the public clocks.
40 Then sit for half an hour and drink our bocks.

II

Now that lilacs are in bloom
She has a bowl of lilacs in her room
And twists one in her fingers while she talks.
"Ah, my friend, you do not know, you do not know
45 What life is, you should hold it in your hands";
(Slowly twisting the lilac stalks)
"You let it flow from you, you let it flow,
And youth is cruel, and has no remorse
And smiles at situations which it cannot see."
50 I smile, of course,
And go on drinking tea.
"Yet with these April sunsets, that somehow recall

My buried life, and Paris in the Spring,
I feel immeasurably at peace, and find the world
To be wonderful and youthful, after all."

The voice returns like the insistent out-of-tune
Of a broken violin on an August afternoon:
"I am always sure that you understand
My feelings, always sure that you feel,
Sure that across the gulf you reach your hand.

You are invulnerable, you have no Achilles' heel.
You will go on, and when you have prevailed
You can say: at this point many a one has failed.

But what have I, but what have I, my friend,
To give you, what can you receive from me?
Only the friendship and the sympathy
Of one about to reach her journey's end.

I shall sit here, serving tea to friends...."

I take my hat: how can I make a cowardly amends
For what she has said to me?
You will see me any morning in the park
Reading the comics and the sporting page.
Particularly I remark An English countess goes upon the stage.
A Greek was murdered at a Polish dance,
Another bank defaulter has confessed.
I keep my countenance, I remain self-possessed
Except when a street piano, mechanical and tired
Reiterates some worn-out common song
With the smell of hyacinths across the garden
Recalling things that other people have desired.
Are these ideas right or wrong?

III

    The October night comes down; returning as before
85   Except for a slight sensation of being ill at ease
    I mount the stairs and turn the handle of the door
    And feel as if I had mounted on my hands and knees.

    "And so you are going abroad; and when do you return?
    But that's a useless question.
90   You hardly know when you are coming back,
    You will find so much to learn."
    My smile falls heavily among the bric-à-brac.

    "Perhaps you can write to me."
    My self-possession flares up for a second;
95   *This* is as I had reckoned.
    "I have been wondering frequently of late
    (But our beginnings never know our ends!)
    Why we have not developed into friends."
    I feel like one who smiles, and turning shall remark
100   Suddenly, his expression in a glass.
    My self-possession gutters; we are really in the dark.

    "For everybody said so, all our friends,
    They all were sure our feelings would relate
    So closely! I myself can hardly understand.
105   We must leave it now to fate.
    You will write, at any rate.
    Perhaps it is not too late.
    I shall sit here, serving tea to friends."

    And I must borrow every changing shape
110   To find expression... dance, dance
    Like a dancing bear,

Cry like a parrot, chatter like an ape.
Let us take the air, in a tobacco trance—
Well! and what if she should die some afternoon,
Afternoon grey and smoky, evening yellow and rose;   115
Should die and leave me sitting pen in hand
With the smoke coming down above the housetops;
Doubtful, for quite a while
Not knowing what to feel or if I understand
Or whether wise or foolish, tardy or too soon...   120
Would she not have the advantage, after all?
This music is successful with a "dying fall"
Now that we talk of dying—
And should I have the right to smile?

Morning at the Window

    They are rattling breakfast plates in basement kitchens,
    And along the trampled edges of the street
    I am aware of the damp souls of housemaids
    Sprouting despondently at area gates.

5   The brown waves of fog toss up to me
    Twisted faces from the bottom of the street,
    And tear from a passer-by with muddy skirts
    An aimless smile that hovers in the air
    And vanishes along the level of the roofs.

The Boston Evening Transcript

The readers of the *Boston Evening Transcript*
Sway in the wind like a field of ripe corn.

When evening quickens faintly in the street,
Wakening the appetites of life in some
And to others bringing the *Boston Evening Transcript*, 5
I mount the steps and ring the bell, turning
Wearily, as one would turn to nod good-bye to
    Rochefoucauld,
If the street were time and he at the end of the street,
And I say, "Cousin Harriet, here is the *Boston Evening
    Transcript.*"

Aunt Helen

Miss Helen Slingsby was my maiden aunt,
And lived in a small house near a fashionable square
Cared for by servants to the number of four.
Now when she died there was silence in heaven
5　And silence at her end of the street.
The shutters were drawn and the undertaker wiped his feet—
He was aware that this sort of thing had occurred before.
The dogs were handsomely provided for,
But shortly afterwards the parrot died too.
10　The Dresden clock continued ticking on the mantelpiece,
And the footman sat upon the dining-table
Holding the second housemaid on his knees—
Who had always been so careful while her mistress lived.

Cousin Nancy

Miss Nancy Ellicott
Strode across the hills and broke them,
Rode across the hills and broke them—
The barren New England hills—
Riding to hounds
Over the cow-pasture.

Miss Nancy Ellicott smoked
And danced all the modern dances;
And her aunts were not quite sure how they felt about it,
But they knew that it was modern.

Upon the glazen shelves kept watch
Matthew and Waldo, guardians of the faith,
The army of unalterable law.

Mr. Apollinax

WHEN Mr. Apollinax visited the United States
His laughter tinkled among the teacups.
I thought of Fragilion, that shy figure among the birch-trees,
And of Priapus in the shrubbery
5   Gaping at the lady in the swing.
In the palace of Mrs. Phlaccus, at Professor
         Channing-Cheetah's
He laughed like an irresponsible foetus.
His laughter was submarine and profound
Like the old man of the sea's
10 Hidden under coral islands
Where worried bodies of drowned men drift down in the
         green silence,
Dropping from fingers of surf.
I looked for the head of Mr. Apollinax rolling under a chair
Or grinning over a screen
15 With seaweed in its hair.
I heard the beat of centaur's hoofs over the hard turf
As his dry and passionate talk devoured the afternoon.
"He is a charming man"—"But after all what did he mean?"—
"His pointed ears... He must be unbalanced,"—
20 "There was something he said that I might have challenged."
Of dowager Mrs. Phlaccus, and Professor and Mrs. Cheetah
I remember a slice of lemon, and a bitten macaroon.

Conversation Galante

I observe: "Our sentimental friend the moon!
Or possibly (fantastic, I confess)
It may be Prester John's balloon
Or an old battered lantern hung aloft
To light poor travellers to their distress."　　　　5
She then: "How you digress!"

And I then: "Some one frames upon the keys
That exquisite nocturne, with which we explain
The night and moonshine; music which we seize
To body forth our vacuity."　　　　10
She then: "Does this refer to me?"
"Oh no, it is I who am inane."

"You, madam, are the eternal humorist,
The eternal enemy of the absolute,
Giving our vagrant moods the slightest twist!　　　　15
With your air indifferent and imperious
At a stroke our mad poetics to confute—"
And—"Are we then so serious?"

Hysteria

As she laughed I was aware of becoming involved in her laughter and being part of it, until her teeth were only accidental stars with a talent for squad-drill. I was drawn in by short gasps, inhaled at each momentary recovery, lost finally in the dark caverns of her throat, bruised by the ripple of unseen muscles. An elderly waiter with trembling hands was hurriedly spreading a pink and white checked cloth over the rusty green iron table, saying: "If the lady and gentleman wish to take their tea in the garden, if the lady and gentleman wish to take their tea in the garden..." I decided that if the shaking of her breasts could be stopped, some of the fragments of the afternoon might be collected, and I concentrated my attention with careful subtlety to this end.

Made in the USA
Columbia, SC
11 June 2021